501 Quotes about Life

Funny, Inspirational and Motivational Quotes

M.Prefontaine

https://twitter.com/quotes4livingby

https://www.facebook.com/QuotesForLivingby/

M. Prefontaine has asserted his moral right to be identified as the author of this work in accordance with the Copyright, Designs and Patents Act 1988.
All rights reserved. No part of this publication may be reproduced, stored in a retrieval system, or transmitted in any form or by any means, electronic, mechanical, photocopying or otherwise without the prior permission of the copyright owner.

INTRODUCTION

Words have power and none more so than some of the most powerful quotes from some of the great minds of history.

Thoughts expressed succinctly can inspire and motivate individuals to change their lives, they can get a message across and they can provide insight.

This is a collection of life quotes selected by the author which is designed to inspire, motivate and amuse. They are a diverse collection ranging from Socrates to Mae West and provide many different viewpoints.

You can just pick this book up anytime and carry on where you left off last time. It is for those who want to pep up a speech, a presentation or an email and for those who just want to jump start their brains with thought provoking or amusing quotations.

I hope this book will prove useful, amusing and the quotes will resonate with you.

1.
Imagination is everything. It is the previ
of life's coming attractions.
Albert Einstein

2.
It's not enough to be busy. So are the ants.
The question is what are we busy about.
Henry David Thoreau

3.
Do not go where the path may lead, go
instead where there is no path and leave a
trail.
Ralph Waldo Emerson

4.
Rock bottom became the solid foundation
on which I rebuilt my life.
J.K. Rowling

5.
My mistakes are my life.
Samuel Beckett

6.
Life does not consist mainly, or even
largely, of facts and happenings. It consists
mainly of the storm of thought that is
forever flowing through one's head.
Mark Twain

7.
Inch by inch. Life is a cinch. Yard by yard.
Life is hard.
John Updike

8.
Life is all memory except for the one present moment that goes by so quick you can hardly catch it going.
Tennessee Williams

9.
Looking good and dressing well is a necessity. Having a purpose in life is not.
Oscar Wilde

10.
Life would be infinitely happier if we could only be born at the age of eighty and gradually approach eighteen.
Mark Twain

11.
Time
Like a petal in the wind
Flows softly by
As old lives are taken
New ones begin
A continual chain
Which lasts throughout eternity
Every life but a minute in time
But each of equal importance
Cindy Cheney

12.
If you don't know where you're going, any road'll take you there.
George Harrison

13.
Live your own life, for you will die your own death.
Latin Proverb

14.
No persons are more frequently wrong, than those who will not admit they are wrong.
François de La Rochefoucauld

15.
Without music, life would be a mistake.... I would only believe in a God who knew how to dance.
Friedrich Nietzsche

16.
Never doubt that a small group of thoughtful, committed, citizens can change the world. Indeed, it is the only thing that ever has.
Margaret Mead

17.
What is human life? The first third a good time; the rest remembering about it.
Mark Twain

18.
Anyone who lives within their means suffers from a lack of imagination.
Oscar Wilde

19.
Never mistake knowledge for wisdom. One helps you make a living; the other helps you make a life.
Sandra Carey

20.
A life spent making mistakes is not only more honorable, but more useful than a life spent doing nothing.
George Bernard Shaw

21.
The best index to a person's character is how he treats people who can't do him any good, and how he treats people who can't fight back.
Abigail Van Buren

22.
Live life so completely that when death comes to you like a thief in the night, there will be nothing left for him to steal.
Anon

23.
The flower that blooms in adversity is the rarest and most beautiful of all.
Walt Disney Company, Mulan

24.
I don't know the question, but sex is definitely the answer.
Woody Allen

25.
Life can only be understood backwards;
but it must be lived forwards.
Søren Kierkegaard

26.
It is said that your life flashes before your eyes just before you die. That is true, it's called Life.
Terry Pratchett

27.
When I look back on all these worries, I remember the story of the old man who said on his deathbed that he had had a lot of trouble in his life, most of which had never happened
Winston Churchill

28.
Two possibilities exist: either we are alone in the Universe or we are not. Both are equally terrifying.
Arthur C. Clarke

29.
Life's under no obligation to give us what we expect.
Margaret Mitchell

30.
The more I see, the less I know for sure.
John Lennon

31.
Don't worry about life, you're not going to survive it anyway
Anon

32.
I think of life as a good book. The further you get into it, the more it begins to make sense.
Harold Kushner

33.
If cats looked like frogs we'd realize what nasty, cruel little bastards they are. Style. That's what people remember.
Terry Pratchett

34.
Do I not destroy my enemies when I make them my friends?
Abraham Lincoln

35.
All of the top achievers I know are life-long learners... Looking for new skills, insights, and ideas. If they're not learning, they're not growing... not moving toward excellence.
Denis Waitley

36.
The true soldier fights not because he hates what is in front of him, but because he loves what is behind him.
G.K. Chesterton

37.
This is your life and it's ending one moment at a time.
Chuck Palahniuk

38.
If I had to live my life again, I'd make the same mistakes, only sooner.
Tallulah Bankhead

39.
Biology gives you a brain. Life turns it into a mind.
Jeffrey Eugenides

40.
Don't try to make life a mathematics problem with yourself in the center and everything coming out equal. When you're good, bad things can still happen. And if you're bad, you can still be lucky.
Barbara Kingsolver

41.
I lived in solitude in the country and noticed how the monotony of a quiet life stimulates the creative mind.
Albert Einstein

42.
Advice is what we ask for when we already know the answer but wish we didn't.
Erica Jong

43.
I have found that if you love life, life will love you back.
Arthur Rubinstein.

44.
Life has no rehearsals, only performances.
Anon

45.
Uncertainty is the only certainty there is, and knowing how to live with insecurity is the only security.
John Allen Paulos

46.
Life is like an onion: you peel it off one layer at a time, and sometimes you weep.
Carl Sandburg

47.
The paradox of courage is that a man must be a little careless of his life even in order to keep it.
G. K. Chesterton

48.
Bitterness is like cancer. It eats upon the host. But anger is like fire. It burns it all clean.
Maya Angelou.

49.
You have enemies? Good. That means you've stood up for something, sometime in your life.
Winston Churchill

50.
You cannot solve a problem with the same mind that created it.
Albert Einstein

51.
You gain strength, courage and confidence by every experience in which you really stop to look fear in the face.
Eleanor Roosevelt.

52.
Teach this triple truth to all: A generous heart, kind speech, and a life of service and compassion are the things which renew humanity.
Buddha

53.
Whether you believe you can do a thing or not, you are right.
Henry Ford.

54.
Life has no meaning the moment you lose the illusion of being eternal.
Jean-Paul Sartre

55.
Life is a flower of which love is the honey.
Victor Hugo

56.
Life is ours to be spent, not to be saved.
D. H. Lawrence

57.
Life is mostly froth and bubble, Two things stand like stone, Kindness in another's trouble, Courage in your own.
Adam Lindsay Gordon

58.
All that we see and seem is but a dream within a dream.
Edgar Allan Poe

59.
Life would be tragic if it weren't funny.
Stephen Hawking

60.
There is no more fatal blunderer than he who consumes the greater part of his life getting his living.
Henry David Thoreau

61.
Life's tragedy is that we get old too soon and wise too late.
Benjamin Franklin

62.
The life of every man is a diary in which he means to write one story, and writes another.
James Matthew Barrie

63.
Today you are You, that is truer than true. There is no one alive who is Youer than You.
Dr. Seuss

64.
You can do anything, but not everything.
David Allen

65.
Life is never fair, and perhaps it is a good thing for most of us that it is not.
Oscar Wilde

66.
Perfection is achieved, not when there is nothing more to add, but when there is nothing left to take away.
Antoine de Saint-Exupéry

67.
The biggest adventure you can take is to live the life of your dreams.
Oprah Winfrey

68.
I find my life is a lot easier the lower I keep everyone's expectations.
Bill Watterson

69
Life is never easy for those who dream.
Robert James Waller

70.
Courage is not the absence of fear, but rather the judgement that something else is more important than fear.
Ambrose Redmoon

71.
The third-rate mind is only happy when it is thinking with the majority. The second-rate mind is only happy when it is thinking with the minority. The first-rate mind is only happy when it is thinking.
A. A. Milne

72.
To the man who only has a hammer, everything he encounters begins to look like a nail.
Abraham Maslow

73.
Each player must accept the cards life deals him or her: but once they are in hand, he or she alone must decide how to play the cards in order to win the game.
Voltaire

74.
Life consists in what a man is thinking of all day.
Ralph Waldo Emerson

75.
A wise man gets more use from his enemies than a fool from his friends.
Baltasar Gracian

76.
The price of anything is the amount of life you exchange for it.
Henry David Thoreau

77.
The real voyage of discovery consists not in seeking new lands but seeing with new eyes.
Marcel Proust

78.
Always forgive your enemies; nothing annoys them so much.
Oscar Wilde

79.
Believe those who are seeking the truth. Doubt those who find it.
André Gide

80.
Most people fail in life because they major in minor things.
Anthony Robbins

81.
It is the mark of an educated mind to be able to entertain a thought without accepting it.
Aristotle

82.
Don't ever wrestle with a pig. You'll both get dirty, but the pig will enjoy it.
Cale Yarborough

83.
In life as in dance: Grace glides on blistered feet.
Alice Abrams

84.
The cure for boredom is curiosity. There is no cure for curiosity.
Ellen Parr

85.
The most important things in life aren't things.
Anthony J. D'Angelo

86.
The trouble with the rat race is that even if you win, you're still a rat.
Lily Tomlin

87.
Never attribute to malice that which is adequately explained by stupidity.
Robert J Hanlon

88.
If God were suddenly condemned to live the life which He has inflicted upon men, He would kill Himself.
Alexandre Dumas Père

89.
There are two great days in a person's life -
- the day we are born and the day we
discover why.
William Barclay

90.
If a man neglects education, he walks lame
to the end of his life.
Plato

91.
Who among us hasn't envied a cat's ability
to ignore the cares of daily life and to relax
completely?
Karen Brademeyer

92.
He felt that his whole life was some kind of
dream and he sometimes wondered whose
it was and whether they were enjoying it.
Douglas Adams

93.
Good friends, good books and a sleepy
conscience: this is the ideal life.
Mark Twain

94.
You will find as you look back upon your
life that the moments when you have really
lived are the moments when you have done
things in the spirit of love.
Henry Drummond

95.
I would rather live my life as if there is a God and die to find out there isn't, than live my life as if there isn't and die to find out there is.
Albert Camus

96.
Life is one fool thing after another whereas love is two fool things after each other.
Oscar Wilde

97.
Beginning today, treat everyone you meet as if they were going to be dead by midnight. Extend to them all the care, kindness, and understanding you can muster, and do it with no thought of any reward. Your life will never be the same again.
Og Mandino

98.
Life shrinks or expands in proportion to one's courage.
Anais Nin

99.
Life isn't about finding yourself. Life is about creating yourself.
George Bernard Shaw

100.
Life is a dream for the wise, a game for the fool, a comedy for the rich, a tragedy for the poor.
Sholom Aleichem

101.
Earth provides enough to satisfy every man's needs, but not every man's greed.
Mahatma Gandhi

102.
Man is a complex being: he makes deserts bloom - and lakes die.
Gil Scott-Heron

103.
Where do we record the passing of wildlife? Who mourns the silent deaths of the small?
O.R. Melling

104.
I'm not afraid of death; I just don't want to be there when it happens.
Woody Allen

105.
Death ends a life, not a relationship.
Mitch Albom

106.
Every man has his secret sorrows which the world knows not; and often times we call a man cold when he is only sad.
Henry Wadsworth Longfellow

107.
Success is walking from failure to failure with no loss of enthusiasm.
Winston Churchill

108.
It is better to be hated for what you are than to be loved for what you are not.
André Gide

109.
Life is what happens to you while you're busy making other plans.
Allen Saunders

110.
Things change. And friends leave. Life doesn't stop for anybody.
Stephen Chbosky

111.
Life is spectacular. Forget the dark things. Take a drink and let time wash them away to where ever time washes away to.
Tim Tharp

112.
Life is 10% what happens to us and 90% how we react to it.
Dennis P. Kimbro

113.
Look at the sparrows; they do not know what they will do in the next moment. Let us literally live from moment to moment.
Mahatma Gandhi

114.
Courage is the first of human qualities because it is the quality which guarantees all others.
Winston Churchill

115.
To deny people their human rights is to challenge their very humanity.
Nelson Mandela

116.
Most great people have attained their greatest success just one step beyond their greatest failure.
Napoleon Hill

117.
Know where to find the information and how to use it - That's the secret of success.
Albert Einstein

118.
The secret of all victory lies in the organization of the non-obvious.
Marcus Aurelius

119.
Pay no attention to what the critics say; no statue has ever been erected to a critic.
Jean Sibelius

120.
There is only one thing that makes a dream impossible to achieve: the fear of failure.
Paulo Coelho

121.
Great people, no matter their field, have similar habits. Learn them and use them in your own quest for greatness.
Paula Andress

122.
Obstacles are those things you see when you take your eyes off the goal.
Henry Ford

123.
Choose a job you love, & you will never have to work a day in your life.
Confucius

124.
You choose the life you live. If you don't like it, it's on you to change it because no one else is going to do it for you.
Kim Kiyosaki

125.
Greatness is not found in possessions, power, position, or prestige. It is discovered in goodness, humility, service, & character.
WA Ward

126
Critical feedback is the breakfast of champions. Defensiveness is the dinner of losers.
Dharmesh Shah

127.
Don't be pushed by your problems. Be led by your dreams.
Ralph Waldo Emerson

128.
You have not lived today until you have done something for someone who can never repay you.
John Bunyan

129.
Success consists of going from failure to failure without loss of enthusiasm.
Winston Churchill

130.
If it isn't a little scary it probably isn't worth your time.
Ted Murphy

131.
If you worry about what might be, and wonder what might have been, you will ignore what is.
Anon

132.
If you are honest, truthful, and transparent, people trust you. If people trust you, you have no grounds for fear, suspicion or jealousy.
Dalai Lama

133.
Don't let your happiness depend on something you may lose.
C. S. Lewis

134.
Your mind is like water, when agitated it becomes difficult to see but if allowed to settle, the answer becomes clear.
Tsem Tulku Rinpoche

135.
I learned that courage was not the absence of fear, but the triumph over it.
Nelson Mandela

136.
Nothing is impossible, the word itself says 'I'm possible.'
Audrey Hepburn

137.
Eventually all things fall into place. Until then, laugh at the confusion, live for the moments, and know everything happens for a reason.
Albert Schweitzer

138.
If you're never scared or embarrassed or hurt, it means you never take any chances.
Julia Sorel

139.
If you can't find the key to success, pick the lock.
Anon

140.
Life has to be given a meaning because of the obvious fact that it has no meaning.
Henry Miller

141.
The art of love... is largely the art of persistence.
Albert Ellis

142.
Look at the stars. See their beauty. And in that beauty, see yourself.
Draya Mooney

143.
Out of suffering have emerged the strongest souls; the most massive characters are seared with scars
Kahlil Gibran

144.
Do not pray for an easy life, pray for the strength to endure a difficult one.
Bruce Lee

145.
Accept responsibility for your life. Know that it is you who will get you where you want to go, no one else.
Les Brown

146.
What you get by achieving your goals is not as important as what you become by achieving your goals.
Goethe

147.
Remember that happiness is a way of travel, not a destination.
Roy Goodman

148.

I have never let my schooling interfere with my education.
Mark Twain

149.
Motivation is a fire from within. If someone else tries to light that fire under you, chances are it will burn very briefly.
Stephen Covey

150.
Unless you try to do something beyond what you have already mastered, you will never grow.
Ralph Waldo Emerson

151.
A successful man is one who can lay a firm foundation with the bricks others have thrown at him
David Brinkley

152.
The successful warrior is the average man, with laser-like focus.
Bruce Lee

153.
A year from now you will wish you had started today.
Karen Lamb

154.
Those who lack the courage will always find a philosophy to justify it.
Albert Camus

155.
It is better to die on your feet than to live on your knees.
Emiliano Zapata

156.
Take chances, make mistakes. That's how you grow. Pain nourishes your courage. You have to fail in order to practice being brave.
Mary Tyler Moore

157.
The difference between stumbling blocks and stepping stones is how you use them.
Anon

158.
If someone tells you, "You can't" they really mean, "I can't.
Sean Stephenson

159.
When I do good, I feel good. When I do bad, I feel bad. That's my religion.
Abraham Lincoln

160.
All things are difficult before they are easy.
Thomas Fuller

161.
I believe that imagination is stronger than knowledge. That myth is more potent than history. That dreams are more powerful than facts. That hope always triumphs over experience. That laughter is the only cure for grief. And I believe that love is stronger than death.
Robert Fulghum

162.
Yesterday is not ours to recover, but tomorrow is ours to win or lose.
Lyndon B. Johnson

163.
Believe that life is worth living and your belief will help create the fact.
William James

164.
In order to succeed, your desire for success should be greater than your fear of failure.
Bill Cosby

165.
The only way to do great work is to love what you do. If you haven't found it yet, keep looking. Don't settle.
Steve Jobs

166.
We learn something from everyone who passes through our lives. Some lessons are painful, some are painless. But, all are priceless.
Anon

167.
Though no one can go back and make a brand new start, anyone can start from now and make a brand new ending.
Carl Bard

168.
Just remember there is someone out there that is more than happy with less than what you have.
Anon

169.
You must give everything to make your life as beautiful as the dreams that dance in your imagination.
Roman Payne

170.
To live a creative life, we must lose our fear of being wrong.
Anon

171.
Things work out best for those who make the best of how things work out.
John Wooden

172.
Just when you think it can't get any worse, it can. And just when you think it can't get any better, it can.
Nicholas Sparks

173.
Try not to become a person of success, but rather try to become a person of value.
Albert Einstein

174.
Great minds discuss ideas; average minds discuss events; small minds discuss people.
Eleanor Roosevelt

175.
I have not failed. I've just found 10,000 ways that won't work.
Thomas A. Edison

176.
The whole secret of a successful life is to find out what is one's destiny to do, and then do it.
Henry Ford

177.
The ones who are crazy enough to think they can change the world, are the ones who do.
Anon

178.
Don't raise your voice, improve your argument.
Anon

179.
The meaning of life is to find your gift. The purpose of life is to give it away.
Pablo Picasso

180.
The distance between insanity and genius is measured only by success.
Bruce Feirstein

181.
Don't be afraid to give up the good to go for the great.
John D. Rockefeller

182.
Knowledge is being aware of what you can do. Wisdom is knowing when not to do it.
Anon

183.
Success is the sum of small efforts, repeated day-in and day-out.
Robert Collier

184.
People often say that motivation doesn't last. Well, neither does bathing--that's why we recommend it daily.
Zig Ziglar

185.
You've got to get up every morning with determination if you're going to go to bed with satisfaction.
George Lorimer

186.
I attribute my success to this: I never gave or took any excuse.
Florence Nightingale

187.
The most difficult thing is the decision to act, the rest is merely tenacity.
Amelia Earhart

188.
I've learned that people will forget what you said, people will forget what you did, but people will never forget how you made them feel.
Maya Angelou

189.
Whatever you can do, or dream you can, begin it. Boldness has genius, power and magic in it.
Johann Wolfgang von Goethe

190.
There is only one way to avoid criticism: do nothing, say nothing, and be nothing.
Aristotle

191.
Believe you can and you're halfway there.
Theodore Roosevelt

192.
We can easily forgive a child who is afraid of the dark; the real tragedy of life is when men are afraid of the light.
Plato

193.
Too many of us are not living our dreams because we are living our fears.
Les Brown

194.
I have been impressed with the urgency of doing. Knowing is not enough; we must apply. Being willing is not enough; we must do.
Leonardo da Vinci

195.
You take your life in your own hands, and what happens? A terrible thing, no one to blame.
Erica Jong

196.
I didn't fail the test. I just found 100 ways to do it wrong.
Benjamin Franklin

197.
It is not what you do for your children, but what you have taught them to do for themselves, that will make them successful human beings.
Ann Landers

198.
I have learned over the years that when one's mind is made up, this diminishes fear.
Rosa Parks

199.
When everything seems to be going against you, remember that the airplane takes off against the wind, not with it.
Henry Ford

200.
Change your thoughts and you change your world.
Norman Vincent Peale

201.
Either write something worth reading or do something worth writing.
Benjamin Franklin

202.
The true meaning of life is to plant trees, under whose shade you do not expect to sit.
Nelson Henderson

203.
Change is not merely necessary to life, it is life.
Alvin Toffler

204.
My world, my Earth is a ruin. A planet spoiled by the human species. We multiplied and fought and gobbled until there was nothing left, and then we died. We controlled neither appetite nor violence; we did not adapt. We destroyed ourselves. But we destroyed the world first.
Ursula K. Le Guin

205.
We're in a giant car heading towards a brick wall and everyone's arguing over where they're going to sit
David Suzuki

206.
Like music and art, love of nature is a common language that can transcend political or social boundaries.
Jimmy Carter

207.
How wonderful it is that nobody need wait a single moment before starting to improve the world.
Anne Frank

208.
You only live once, but if you do it right, once is enough.
Mae West

209.
In three words I can sum up everything I've learned about life: it goes on.
Robert Frost

210.
To live is the rarest thing in the world. Most people exist, that is all.
Oscar Wilde

211.
There are only two ways to live your life. One is as though nothing is a miracle. The other is as though everything is a miracle.
Albert Einstein

212.
Winning isn't everything, but wanting to win is.
Vince Lombardi

213.
Life is like riding a bicycle. To keep your balance, you must keep moving.
Albert Einstein

214.
Your heart is the size of an ocean. Go find yourself in its hidden depths.
Rumi

215.
You will be bitter in life, when you compare yourself with others.Run the race of life at your own pace.
Lailah Gifty Akita

216.
When I stand before God at the end of my life, I would hope that I would not have a single bit of talent left and could say, I used everything you gave me.
Erma Bombeck

217.
Nurture your mind with great thoughts. To believe in the heroic makes heroes.
Benjamin Disraeli

218.
The difference between a successful person and others is not lack of strength not a lack of knowledge but rather a lack of will.
Vince Lombardi

219.
You must not lose faith in humanity. Humanity is an ocean; if a few drops of the ocean are dirty, the ocean does not become dirty.
Mahatma Gandhi

220.
Failure defeats losers, failure inspires winners.
Robert T. Kiyosaki

221.
If you really want to do something you'll find a way, if you don't you'll find an excuse.
Jim Rohn

222.
Sometimes the best thing you can do is not think, not wonder, not imagine, not obsess. Just breathe and have faith that everything will work out for the best.
Anon

223.
I heard what you said. I'm not the silly romantic you think. I don't want the heavens or the shooting stars. I don't want gemstones or gold. I have those things already. I want...a steady hand. A kind soul. I want to fall asleep, and wake, knowing my heart is safe. I want to love, and be loved.
Shana Abe

224.
Two things define you. Your patience when you have nothing, your attitude when you have everything.
Anon

225.
The biggest mistake you'll ever make is letting people stay in your life for longer than they deserve.
Anon

226.
You don't have to be great to start, but you have to start to be great.
Zig Ziglar

227.
In the middle of every difficulty lies opportunity.
Albert Einstein

228.
You were born with the ability to change someone's life – don't ever waste it.
Dale Partridge

229.
There are no secrets to success. It is the result of preparation, hard work and learning from failure.
Colin Powell

230.
Life is accumulative – Either our errors accumulate to what we don't get, or our wise decisions accumulate into what we do get.
Jim Rohn

231
The biggest risk is not taking any risk... In a world that is changing really quickly, the only strategy that is guaranteed to fail is not taking risks.
Mark Zuckerberg

232
Happiness is not achieved by the conscious pursuit of happiness; it is generally the by-product of other activities.
Aldous Huxley

233.
Failure is a prerequisite for great success. If you want to succeed faster, double your rate of failure.
Brian Tracy

234.
Just Remember: The people that say, "Your dreams are impossible" have already quit on theirs.
Grant Cardone

235.
The only wealth which you will keep forever is the wealth you have given away.
Marcus Aurelius

236.
Water runs if you try to grasp it, but pours onto an open hand.
The Silver Elves

237.
Love doesn't just sit there, like a stone, it has to be made, like bread; remade all the time, made new.
Ursula K. Le Guin

238.
The end is not the reward; the path you take, the emotions that course through you as you grasp life - that is the reward.
Jamie Magee

239.
It is during our darkest moments that we must focus on the light.
Aristotle

240.
If you don't like something, change it. If you can't change it, change your attitude. Don't complain.
Maya Angelou

241.
We are what we repeatedly do. Excellence, therefore, is not an act but a habit.
Aristotle

242.
Desire is the starting point of all achievement, not a hope, not a wish, but a keen pulsating desire which transcends everything.
Napoleon Hill

243.
Whenever you find yourself on the side of the majority, it's time to pause and reflect.
Mark Twain

244.
If you always put limits on everything you do, physical or anything else, it will spread into your work and into your life. There are no limits. There are only plateaus, and you must not stay there, you must go beyond them.
Bruce Lee

245.
If you set your goals ridiculously high and it's a failure, you will fail above everyone else's success.
James Cameron

246.
The key question to keep asking is, 'Are you spending your time on the right things?' Because time is all you have.
Randy Pausch

247.
Life has many ways of testing a person's will, either by having nothing happen at all or by having everything happen all at once.
Paulo Coelho

248.
You can tell the greatness of a man by what makes him angry.
Abraham Lincoln

249.
Life is a gift, and it offers us the privilege, opportunity, and responsibility to give something back by becoming more.
Tony Robbins

250.
Whatever you want to do, do it now. There are only so many tomorrows.
Michael Landon

251.
We are responsible for what we are, and whatever we wish ourselves to be, we have the power to make ourselves.
Swami Vivekananda

252.
The difference in winning and losing is most often...not quitting.
Walt Disney

253.
You are never too old to set another goal or dream a new dream.
C.S Lewis

254
The next time you feel slightly uncomfortable with the pressure in your life, remember no pressure, no diamonds. Pressure is a part of success.
Eric Thomas

255.
Dont be afraid to stand for what you believe in, even if that means standing alone.
Andy Biersack

256
Challenges are what make life interesting and overcoming them is what makes life meaningful.
Joshua J. Marine

257.
Life is short, live it. Love is rare, grab it.
Anger is bad, dump it. Fear is awful, face it.
Memories are sweet, cherish it.
Anon

258.
Being happy doesn't mean that everything is perfect. It means that you've decided to look beyond the imperfections.
Anon

259.
Don't be afraid of your fears. They're not there to scare you. They're there to let you know that something is worth it.
C. JoyBell C.

260.
The greatness of a man is not in how much wealth he acquires, but in his integrity and his ability to affect those around him positively
Bob Marley

261.
If you want to achieve greatness stop asking for permission.
Anon

262.
If you are not willing to risk the usual you will have to settle for the ordinary.
Jim Rohn

263.
Trust because you are willing to accept the risk, not because it's safe or certain.
Anon

264.
Opportunities don't happen, you create them.
Chris Grosser

265.
If you don't value your time, neither will others. Stop giving away your time and talents-start charging for it.
Kim Garst

266.
If you're going through hell keep going.
Winston Churchill

267.
When you stop chasing the wrong things, you give the right things a chance to catch you.
Lolly Daskal

268.
Happiness is a butterfly, which when pursued, is always beyond your grasp, but which, if you will sit down quietly, may alight upon you.
Nathaniel Hawthorne

269.
There are two types of people who will tell you that you cannot make a difference in this world: those who are afraid to try and those who are afraid you will succeed.
Ray Goforth

270.
Two roads diverged in a wood, and I—I took the one less travelled by, And that has made all the difference.
Robert Frost

271.
Life isn't about getting and having, it's about giving and being.
Kevin Kruse

272.
The two most important days in your life are the day you are born and the day you find out why.
Mark Twain

273.
Ask and it will be given to you; search, and you will find; knock and the door will be opened for you.
Jesus

274.
Go confidently in the direction of your dreams. Live the life you have imagined.
Henry David Thoreau

275.
If you want to lift yourself up, lift up someone else.
Booker T. Washington

276.
Limitations live only in our minds. But if we use our imaginations, our possibilities become limitless.
Jamie Paolinetti

277.
What's money? A man is a success if he gets up in the morning and goes to bed at night and in between does what he wants to do.
Bob Dylan

278.
There are no traffic jams along the extra mile.
Roger Staubach

279.
If you want your children to turn out well, spend twice as much time with them, and half as much money.
Abigail Van Buren

280.
It does not matter how slowly you go as long as you do not stop.
Confucius

281.
Do what you can, where you are, with what you have.
Teddy Roosevelt

282.
Our lives begin to end the day we become silent about things that matter.
Martin Luther King Jr.

283.
It's not the years in your life that count. It's the life in your years.
Abraham Lincoln

284.
Sometimes you have to accept how things are. You can make it easy on yourself, or you can make it hard. The choice is yours.
Susan Mallery

285.
You come to a point in your life where you really don't care what people think about you, you just care what you think about yourself.
Evel Knievel

286.
Don't take advantage of those who love you the most. Love those around you like each day is your last.
Heather Lindsey

287.
Don't cry because it's over, smile because it happened."
Dr. Seuss

288.
The difference between school and life? In school, you're taught a lesson and then given a test. In life, you're given a test that teaches you a lesson.
Tom Bodett

289.
Imperfection is beauty, madness is genius and it is better to be absolutely ridiculous than boring.
Marilyn Monroe

290.
It does not do to dwell on dreams and forget to live.
J.K. Rowling,

291.
One's real life is often the life that one does not lead.
Oscar Wilde

292.
Sometimes the questions are complicated and the answers are simple.
Dr. Seuss

293.
When I was young, I thought that money was the most important thing in life; now that I am old, I know it is.
Oscar Wilde

294.
Finish each day and be done with it. You have done what you could. Some blunders and absurdities no doubt crept in; forget them as soon as you can. Tomorrow is a new day. You shall begin it serenely and with too high a spirit to be encumbered with your old nonsense.
Ralph Waldo Emerson

295.
To love is to risk not being loved in return. To hope is to risk pain. To try is to risk failure, but risk must be taken because the greatest hazard in life is to risk nothing.
Leo Buscaglia

296.
I'm the one that's got to die when it's time for me to die, so let me live my life the way I want to.
Jimi Hendrix,

297.
What most people need to learn in life is how to love people and use things instead of using people and loving things.
Zelda Fitzgerald

298.
But better to get hurt by the truth than comforted with a lie.
Khaled Hosseini

299.
The fear of death follows from the fear of life. A man who lives fully is prepared to die at any time.
Mark Twain

300.
If you want to live a happy life, tie it to a goal, not to people or things.
Albert Einstein

301.
We are all in the gutter, but some of us are looking at the stars.
Oscar Wilde

302.
The roughest road often leads to the top.
Christina Aguilera

303.
Stop worrying about the world ending today. It's already tomorrow in Australia.
Charles Monroe Schulz

304.
I can never read all the books I want; I can never be all the people I want and live all the lives I want. I can never train myself in all the skills I want. And why do I want? I want to live and feel all the shades, tones and variations of mental and physical experience possible in my life. And I am horribly limited.
Sylvia Plath

305.
If things seem under control, you are just not going fast enough.
Mario Andretti

306.
This life's hard, but it's harder if you're stupid.
George V. Higgins

307.
We all have two lives. The second one starts when we realize we only have one.
Tom Hiddleston

308.
The saddest aspect of life right now is that science gathers knowledge faster than society gathers wisdom.
Isaac Asimov

309.
Your time is limited, so don't waste it living someone else's life. Don't be trapped by dogma – which is living with the results of other people's thinking. Don't let the noise of others' opinions drown out your own inner voice. And most important, have the courage to follow your heart and intuition. They somehow already know what you truly want to become. Everything else is secondary.
Steve Jobs

310.
Death must be so beautiful. To lie in the soft brown earth, with the grasses waving above one's head, and listen to silence. To have no yesterday, and no to-morrow. To forget time, to forgive life, to be at peace.
Oscar Wilde

311.
You get in life what you have the courage to ask for.
Oprah Winfrey

312.
Do not read, as children do, to amuse yourself, or like the ambitious, for the purpose of instruction. No, read in order to live.
Gustave Flaubert

313.
Mellow doesn't always make for a good story, but it makes for a good life.
Anne Hathaway

314.
I wanted a perfect ending. Now I've learned, the hard way, that some poems don't rhyme, and some stories don't have a clear beginning, middle, and end. Life is about not knowing, having to change, taking the moment and making the best of it, without knowing what's going to happen next.
Delicious Ambiguity.
Gilda Radner

315.
It's better to cross the line and suffer the consequences than to just stare at the line for the rest of your life.
Anon

316.
What we are today comes from our thoughts of yesterday, and our present thoughts build our life of tomorrow: Our life is the creation of our mind.
Buddha

317.
At one point in your life, you will either have the thing you want or reasons why you don't.
Andy Roddick

318.
There are two primary choices in life: to accept conditions as they exist, or accept the responsibility for changing them.
Denis Waitley

319.
Never make permanent decisions on temporary feelings.
Anon

320.
When I was 5 years old, my mother always told me that happiness was the key to life. When I went to school, they asked me what I wanted to be when I grew up. I wrote down 'happy'. They told me I didn't understand the assignment, and I told them they didn't understand life.
John Lennon

321.
No matter how big your house is, how recent your car is, or how big your bank account is — our graves will always be the same size. Stay humble.
Anon

322.
It is not length of life, but depth of life.
Ralph Waldo Emerson

323.
Time is free, but it's priceless. You can't own it, but you can use it. You can spend it, but you can't keep it. Once you've lost it, you can never get it back.
Harvey MacKay

324.
Life is the art of drawing without an eraser.
John W. Gardner

325.
We all create the person we become by our choices as we go through life. In a real sense, by the time we are adults, we are the sum total of the choices we have made.
Eleanor Roosevelt

326.
My experience of life is that it is not divided up into genres; it's a horrifying, romantic, tragic, comical, science-fiction cowboy detective novel. You know, with a bit of pornography if you're lucky.
Alan Moore

326.
The time you enjoy wasting is not time wasted.
Bertrand Russell

327.
Life wastes itself while we are preparing to live.
Ralph Waldo Emerson

328.
Life has no limitations, except the ones you make.
Les Brown

329.
The most important thing is to enjoy your life—to be happy—it's all that matters.
Audrey Hepburn

330.
Don't save things for a special occasion. Every day of your life is a special occasion.
Thomas S. Monson

331.
When I hear somebody sigh, "Life is hard," I am always tempted to ask, "Compared to what?"
Sydney J. Harris

332.
Time has a wonderful way of showing us what really matters in life.
Anon

333.
Life is really simple, but we insist on making it complicated.
Confucius

334.
I always say don't make plans, make options.
Jennifer Aniston

335.
Pain makes man think. Thought makes man wise. Wisdom makes life endurable.
John Patrick

336.
In life, you are either the passenger or the pilot, it's your decision.
Anon

337.
Before you act, listen. Before you react, think. Before you spend, earn. Before you criticize, wait. Before you pray, forgive. Before you quit, try.
Ernest Hemingway

338.
Nobody realizes that some people expend tremendous energy merely to be normal.
Albert Camus

339.
Only put off until tomorrow what you are willing to die having left undone.
Pablo Picasso

340.
No one really knows why they are alive until they know what they'd die for.
Martin Luther King Jr

341.
Your life does not get better by chance, it gets better by change.
Jim Rohn

342.
We avoid risks in life so we can make it safely to death.
Philosoraptor

343.
The most wasted of all days is one without laughter.
Nicolas Chamfort

344.
Simplicity is the ultimate sophistication.
Leonardo da Vinci

345.
Why didn't I learn to treat everything like it was the last time. My greatest regret was how much I believed in the future.
Jonathan Safran Foer

346.
Everything should be made as simple as possible, but not simpler.
Albert Einstein

347.
Life's challenges are not supposed to paralyze you, they're supposed to help you discover who you are.
Bernice Johnson Reagon

348.
The hardest thing in life is to know which bridge to cross and which to burn.
David Russell

349.
There are few hours in life more agreeable than the hour dedicated to the ceremony known as afternoon tea.
Henry James

350.
Don't part with your illusions. When they are gone you may still exist, but you have ceased to live.
Mark Twain

351.
Only love matters in the bits and pieces of a person's life.
William Trevor

352.
You must understand the whole of life, not just one little part of it. That is why you must read, that is why you must look at the skies, that is why you must sing, and dance, and write poems, and suffer, and understand, for all that is life.
Jiddu Krishnamurti

353.
Among those whom I like or admire, I can find no common denominator, but among those whom I love, I can; all of them make me laugh.
WH Auden

354.
Live to the point of tears.
Albert Camus

355.
Life is all about timing... the unreachable becomes reachable, the unavailable become available, the unattainable... attainable. Have the patience, wait it out It's all about timing.
Stacey Charter

356.
Success is getting what you want, happiness is wanting what you get.
Ingrid Bergman

357.
I go to seek a Great Perhaps.
François Rabelais

358.
Life is a great big canvas, and you should throw all the paint you can on it.
Danny Kaye

359.
That's it baby, if you've got it, flaunt it.
Mel Brooks

360.
Death is not the greatest loss in life. The greatest loss is what dies inside us while we live.
Norman Cousins

361.
The saddest people I've ever met in life are the ones who don't care deeply about anything at all. Passion and satisfaction go hand in hand, and without them, any happiness is only temporary, because there's nothing to make it last.
Nicholas Sparks

362.
Once we are destined to live out our lives in the prison of our mind, our duty is to furnish it well.
Peter Ustinov

363.
All life is an experiment. The more experiments you make the better.
Ralph Waldo Emerson

364.
Things work out best for those who make the best of how things work out.
John Wooden

365.
To know even one life has breathed easier because you have lived - that is to have succeeded.
Ralph Waldo Emerson

366.
The ultimate answer to life, the universe and EVERYTHING is . . . 42!"
Douglas Adams

367.
Don't judge each day by the harvest you reap but by the seeds you plant
Robert Louis Stevenson.

368.
Does the universe exist only for me? It's possible. If so, it's sure going well for me, I must admit.
Bill Gates

369.
Pain is inevitable. Suffering is optional
Haruki Murakami

370.
One's life has value so long as one attributes value to the life of others, by means of love, friendship, and compassion.
Simone de Beauvoir

371.
Life is dull only to dull people.
Anon

372.
You are not in this world to live up to other people's expectations, nor should you feel the world must live up to yours.
Fritz Perl

373
The most common way people give up their power is by thinking they don't have any.
Alice Walker

374.
Life is either a daring adventure or nothing.
Helen Keller.

375.
It is only with the heart that one can see rightly, everything essential is invisible to the eye.
Antoine de Saint-Exupéry

376.
Life without love is a shadow of things that might be.
Neil Gaiman

377.
It's impossible" said pride. "It's risky" said experience. "It's pointless" said reason. "Give it a try" whispered the heart
Jason Santana

378.
Be more concerned with your character than your reputation, because your character is what you really are, while your reputation is merely what others think you are.
John Wooden.

379.
Love life, engage in it, give it all you've got. love it with a passion, because life truly does give back, many times over, what you put into it.
Maya Angelou

380.
Life is partly what we make it, and partly what it is made by the friends we choose.
Tennessee Williams

381.
The harder you fall, the higher you bounce
John Paul Warren

382.
Life is like a box of chocolates. You never know what you're going to get.
Forrest Gump

383.
Change is the essence of life. Be willing to surrender what you are for what you could become.
Reinhold Niebuhr

384.
Dost thou love life? Then do not squander time, for that is the stuff life is made of.
Benjamin Franklin

385.
Take control of your consistent emotions and begin to consciously and deliberately reshape your daily experience of life.
Anthony Robbins

386.
The secret of success is learning how to use pain and pleasure instead of having pain and pleasure use you. If you do that, you're in control of your life. If you don't, life controls you.
Anthony Robbins

387.
The true harvest of my life is intangible - a little star dust caught, a portion of the rainbow I have clutched.
Henry David Thoreau

388.
Reality continues to ruin my life.
Bill Watterson

389.
Unless a life is lived for others, it is not worthwhile.
Mother Teresa of Calcutta

390.
Dreams do come true, if we only wish hard enough. You can have anything in life if you will sacrifice everything else for it.
JM Barrie

391.
The richest man is not he who has the most, but he who needs the least.
Paul Kavanagh

392.
Life is thickly sown with thorns, and I know no other remedy than to pass quickly through them. The longer we dwell on our misfortunes, the greater is their power to harm us.
Voltaire

393.
Do not seek to follow in the footsteps of the men of old; seek what they sought.
Basho

394.
Even if you're on the right track, you'll get run over if you just sit there.
Will Rogers

395.
Those of us we have been true readers all our life fully realize the enormous extension of our being which we owe to authors.
C.S. Lewis

396.
All changes, even the most longed for, have their melancholy; for what we leave behind us is a part of ourselves; we must die to one life before we can enter another.
Anatole France

397.
When we long for life without difficulties, remind us that oaks grow strong in contrary winds and diamonds are made under pressure.
Peter Marshall

398.
I've been absolutely terrified every moment of my life -- and I've never let it keep me from doing a single thing I wanted to do.
Georgia O'Keeffe

399.
Life is a dream for the wise, a game for the fool, a comedy for the rich, a tragedy for the poor.
Sholom Aleichem

400.
Life's tragedy is that we get old too soon and wise too late
Benjamin Franklin

401.
What is important in life is life, and not the result of life.
Johann Wolfgang Von Goethe

402.
The average person living to age 70 has 613, 000 hours of life. This is too long a period not to have fun.
Anon

403.
Every man's life ends the same way. It is only the details of how he lived and how he died that distinguish one man from another.
Ernest Hemingway

404.
The greatest lesson in life is to know that even fools are right sometimes.
Winston Churchill

405.
I sit astride life like a bad rider on a horse. I only owe it to the horse's good nature that I am not thrown off at this very moment.
Ludwig Wittgenstein

406.
People need to be made more aware of the need to work at learning how to live because life is so quick and sometimes it goes away too quickly
Andy Warhol

407.
Life is a zoo in a jungle.
Peter de Vries

408.
It is advisable that a person know at least three things, where they are, where they are going, and what they had best do under the circumstances.
John Ruskin

409.
Just as the wave cannot exist for itself, but is ever a part of the heaving surface of the ocean, so must I never live my life for itself, but always in the experience which is going on around me.
Albert Schweitzer

410.
If you don't design your own life plan, chances are you will fall into someone else's plan and guess what they have planned for you. Not Much.
Jim Rohn

411.
A hundred years from now it will not matter what my bank account was, the sort of house I lived in, or the kind of car I drove...but the world may be different because I was important in the life of a child.
Forest E. Witcraft

412.
You cannot find peace by avoiding life.
Virginia Woolf

413.
We are what we pretend to be, so we must be careful about what we pretend to be.
Kurt Vonnegut

414.
Life is a game. Money is how we keep score.
Ted Turner

415.
Life is a cement trampoline.
Howard Nordberg

416.
God pours life into death and death into life without a drop being spilled
Anon

417.
Following straight lines shortens distances, and also life.
Antonio Porchia

418.
Life is so largely controlled by chance that its conduct can be but a perpetual improvisation.
W. Somerset Maugham

419.
Most important thing in life ... is learning how to fall.
Jeanette Walls

420.
Life is not so bad if you have plenty of luck, a good physique, and not too much imagination.
Christopher Isherwood

421.
Our lives are waves that come up out of the ocean of eternity, break upon the beach of earth, and lapse back to the ocean of eternity. Some are sunlit, some run in storm and rain; one is a quiet ripple, another is a thunderous breaker; and once in many centuries comes a great tidal wave that sweeps over a continent; but all go back to the sea and lie equally level there.
Austin O'Malley

422.
Life is a dream in the night, a fear among fears,
A naked runner lost in a storm of spears.
Arthur Symons

423.
I think everybody should get rich and famous and do everything they ever dreamed of so they can see that it's not the answer.
Jim Carrey

424.
Life is not always a matter of holding good cards, but sometimes, playing a poor hand well.
Jack London

425.
Life will always remain a gamble, with prizes sometimes for the imprudent, and blanks so often to the wise.
Jerome K. Jerome

426.
Life calls the tune, we dance.
John Galsworthy

427.
My formula for living is quite simple. I get up in the morning and I go to bed at night. In between, I occupy myself as best I can.
Cary Grant

428.
Life is a hill that gets steeper the more you climb.
John Updike

429.
A life without cause is a life without effect.
Paul Coelho

430.
My life has a superb cast but I can't figure out the plot.
Ashleigh Brilliant

431.
You fall out of your mother's womb, you crawl across open country under fire, and drop into your grave.
Quentin Crisp

432.
Life, just as we first thought, is playing grownup.
John Updike

433.
The essence of human experience lay not primarily in the peak experiences, the wedding days and triumphs which stood out in the memory like dates circled in red on old calendars, but, rather, in the unself-conscious flow of little things--the weekend afternoon with each member of the family engaged in his or her own pursuit, their crossings and connections casual, dialogues imminently forgettable, but the sum of such hours creating a synergy which was important and eternal.
Dan Simmons

434.
Life is a compromise of what your ego wants to do, what experience tells you to do, and what your nerves let you do.
Bruce Crampton

435.
You're pretending this isn't your life. You think it's going to happen some other time. When you're dead you'll realize you were alive now.
Caryl Churchill

436.
The road is life.
Jack Kerouac

437.
Life has meaning only if one barters it day by day for something other than itself.
Antoine de Saint-Exupery

438.
Life is but a prelude.
Edward Counsel

439.
Life is a moment stolen from eternity.
Eliza Cook

440.
The lives of people are like young trees in a forest. They are being choked by climbing vines. The vines are old thoughts and beliefs planted by dead men.
Sherwood Anderson

441.
**The fine art of Life is to make
Another Soul vibrate with a song of joy.**
Edwin Liebfreed

442.
Live on, survive, for the earth gives forth wonders. It may swallow your heart, but the wonders keep on coming. You stand before them bareheaded, shriven. What is expected of you is attention.
Salman Rushdie

443.
**One word
Frees us of all the weight and pain of life:
That word is love.**
Sophocles

444.
Between a gasp and a sigh, a life can change forever.
Tim Lebbon

445.
Success makes life easier. It doesn't make living easier.
Bruce Springsteen

446.
Maybe all one can do is hope to end up with the right regrets.
Arthur Miller

447.
He who has a why to live can bear almost any how.
Friedrich Nietzsche

448.
Here is the world. Beautiful and terrible things will happen. Don't be afraid.
Frederick Buechner

449.
Life may have no meaning. Or even worse, it may have a meaning of which I disapprove.
Ashleigh Brilliant

450.
The bad news is you're falling through the air, nothing to hang on to, no parachute. The good news is, there's no ground.
Chogyam Trungpa Rinpoche

451.
A ship is safe in harbor, but that's not what ships are for.
William G.T. Shedd

452.
Nobody ever wrote down a plan to be broke, fat, lazy, or stupid. Those things are what happen when you don't have a plan.
Larry Winget

453.
All the world is made of faith, and trust, and pixie dust.
J.M. Barrie, Peter Pan

454.
Your life is not a problem to be solved but a gift to be opened.
Wayne Muller

455.
Our ability to grow is directly proportional to an ability to entertain the uncomfortable.
Twyla Tharp

456.
My favorite things in life don't cost any money. It is really clear that the most precious resource we all have is time.
Steve Jobs

457.
There is a time early in life when there seem to be countless reasons for happiness, and then you discover your mom is making them up.
Robert Brault

458.
He who has nothing to die for has nothing to live for.
Moroccan Proverb

459.
Life is like eating artichokes; you have got to go through so much to get so little.
Thomas Aloysius Dorgan

460.
When we remember we are all mad, the mysteries disappear and life stands explained.
Mark Twain

461.
Life is a sexually transmitted disease and there is a 100% mortality rate.
R.D. Laing

462.
Some journeys in life can only be traveled alone
Ken Poirot

463.
Life is a horizontal fall.
Jean Cocteau

464.
I say to my child, I will explain to you as much of life as I can, but you must remember that there is a part of life for which you are the explanation.
Robert Brault

465.
In the book of life, the answers aren't in the back.
Charlie Brown

466.
If A equals success, then the formula is: A = X + Y + Z, where X is work, Y is play, and Z is keep your mouth shut.
Albert Einstein

467.
My friend asked me the essence of life and I smiled.
Mike Dolan

468.
The universe is like a safe to which there is a combination. But the combination is locked up in the safe.
Peter De Vries

469.
The best revenge is massive success.
Frank Sinatra

470.
Three things you cannot recover in life: the WORD after it's said, the MOMENT after it's missed and the TIME after it's gone. Be Careful!
Anon

471.
And those who were seen dancing were thought to be insane by those who could not hear the music.
Friedrich Nietzsche

472.
Anything or anyone that does not bring you alive is too small for you.
David Whyte

473.
Life is like photography. You need the negatives to develop.
Ziad K Abdelnour

474.
Do not feel lonely, the entire universe is within you.
Rumi

475.
The world needs dreamers and the world needs doers But above all the world needs dreamers who do.
Sarah Breathnach

476.
To see a World in a Grain of Sand And a Heaven in a Wild Flower, Hold Infinity in the palm of your hand And Eternity in an hour.
William Blake

477.
Light always trumps the dark.you can stick a candle into the dark but you cant stick the dark into a candle.
Jodi Picoult

478.
The best place to find a helping hand is at the end of your own arm.
Swedish Proverb

479.
A good heart and a good head are always a formidable combination.
Nelson Mandela

480.
Creativity is contagious. Pass it on.
Albert Einstein

481.
Be the change you wish to see in the world.
Mahatma Gandhi

482.
There are two ways to slide easily through life: to believe everything or to doubt everything; both ways save us from thinking.
Alfred Korzybski

483.
You may have to fight a battle more than once to win it.
Margaret Thatcher

484.
The minute that you're not learning I believe you're dead.
Jack Nicholson

485.
I hated every minute of training, but I said, 'Don't quit. Suffer now and live the rest of your life as a champion.
Muhammad Ali

486.
Someone is sitting in the shade today because someone planted a tree a long time ago.
Warren Buffet

487.
Eighty percent of success is showing up.
Woody Allen

488.
Dreaming, after all, is a form of planning.
Gloria Steinem

489.
One child, one teacher, one book, one pen can change the world.
Malala Yousafzai

490.
You never really learn much from hearing yourself talk.
George Clooney

491.
The first step to getting the things you want out of life is this: Decide what you want.
Ben Stein

492.
Focusing your life solely on making a buck shows a certain poverty of ambition. It asks too little of yourself. Because it's only when you hitch your wagon to something larger than yourself that you realize your true potential.
Barack Obama

493.
Find out who you are and be that person. That's what your soul was put on this Earth to be. Find that truth, live that truth and everything else will come.
Ellen Degeneres

494.
When a defining moment comes along, you define the moment, or the moment defines you.
Kevin Costner

495.
The difference between ordinary and extraordinary is that little extra.
Jimmy Johnson

The great gift of human beings is that we have the power of empathy.
Meryl Streep

497.
The harder I work, the luckier I get.
Gary Player

498.
Success is walking from failure to failure with no loss of enthusiasm.
Winston Churchill

499.
Remarkable is a choice.
Seth Godin

500.
The man who moves a mountain begins by carrying away small stones.
Confucius

501.
Life does not cease to be funny when people die any more than it ceases to be serious when people laugh.
George Bernard Shaw

ONE LAST THING...

If you enjoyed this book or found it useful I'd be very grateful if you'd post a short review on Amazon. Your support really does make a difference and I read all the reviews personally so I can get your feedback and make this book even better. If you'd like to leave a review then all you need to do is click the review link on this book's page on Amazon.

Other books by the author

The Big Book of Quotes

The Book of Best Sports Quotes

Many thanks for your support

Printed in Great Britain
by Amazon